# First Sticker Book
# Animals

Illustrated by Cecilia Johansson

## Contents

There are lots of stickers at the back
of this book for you to stick on each page.

Words by Jessica Greenwell
Designed by Meg Dobbie and Hanri van Wyk

1

# Dusty desert

It's hot and dry in the Australian desert. Where could you put a kangaroo and some hopping mice?

# In the farmyard

It's feeding time on the farm. Can you find a place for a hungry horse?

# Grassy plains

It's very hot in the African grasslands. Where could you put a muddy hippopotamus?

# A snowy world

It's a cold, icy day in the Arctic. Can you put a polar bear on the snow?

# Icy waters

In the Antarctic the water is freezing cold. Where could you put a swimming penguin and some ice fish?

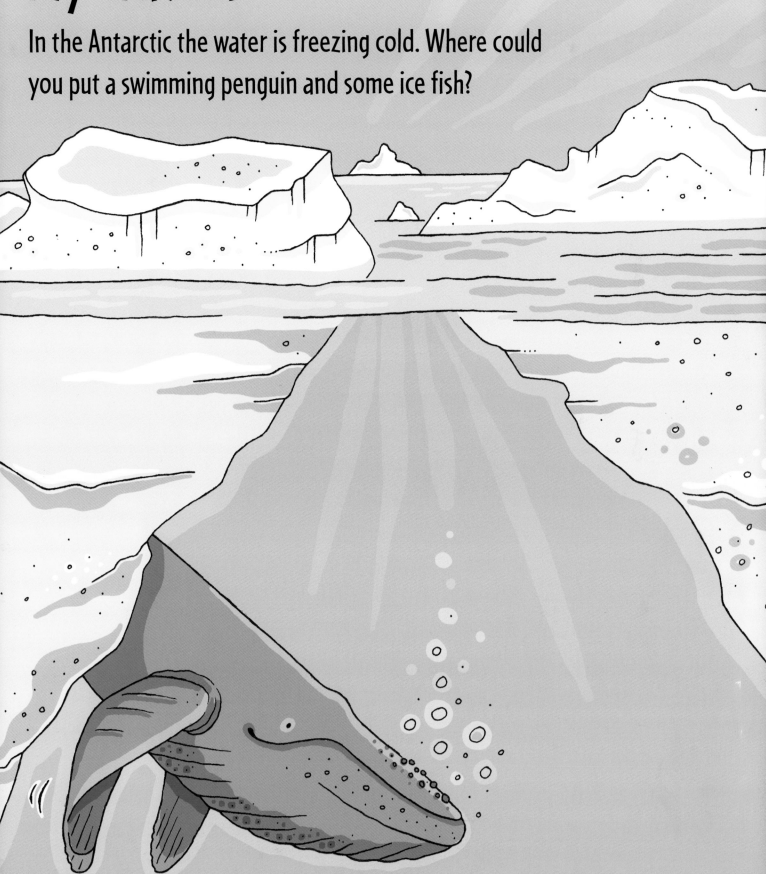

# Animals at home

Pets love to be outside in the springtime. Can you find a place for a puppy chasing a butterfly?

# In the rainforest

The rainforest is full of tall trees and big plants.
Where could you stick a slithering snake?

# Under the sea

There are lots of animals in the deep blue sea.
Where could a crab crawl and a sea horse swim?

# Baby animal puzzle

Can you help each animal find its baby?

Possum

Kangaroo

Wombat

Dingo

Parakeet

Emu

Kookaburras

Goanna

Hopping mice

Wallaby

# In the farmyard – page 4

Duck

Ducklings

Chicks

Cow

Foal

Hen

Sheep

Horse

Goat

Donkey

Hen

Lambs

Chick

Bull

# Grassy plains – page 6

Guinea fowl

Hippopotamuses

Dung beetle

Zebras

Gazelle

Cheetah

Giraffe

Leopard

Giraffe

Rhinoceros

Baby elephant

Lion

Lioness

Lion cubs

Ostrich

Elephant

# A snowy world – page 8

Polar bear cubs

Arctic hare

Snowy owls

Arctic foxes

Walruses

Polar bear

# Icy waters – page 9

Penguins

Seals

Ice fish

# Animals at home

Worm

Cat

Birds

Rabbit

Cat

Mole

Frog

Snail

Mouse

Dog

Puppy

Kitten

Mice

Caterpillar

Birds

Guinea pigs

Bee

# In the rainforest – page 12

Jaguar

Tree frogs

Monkey

Sloths

Butterflies

Tree frogs

Alligator

Armadillo

Snakes

Toucan

Parrots

Tapir

# Under the sea – page 14

Jellyfish

Dolphin

Angelfish

Crab

Sea anemone

Shark

Starfish

Rainbow fish

Sea turtles

Dolphin

Octopus

Squid

Clown fish

Sea horse